The Way Home

The Way Home
a Princess Story

MAX LUCADO
ILLUSTRATED BY TRISTEN ELWELL

A Division of Thomas Nelson Publishers
Since 1798

www.thomasnelson.com

Published in Nashville, Tennessee, by Tommy Nelson®, a Division
of Thomas Nelson, Inc.

Tommy Nelson® books may be purchased in bulk for educational,
business, fundraising, or sales promotional use. For information,
please e-mail SpecialMarkets@ThomasNelson.com.

Library of Congress Cataloging-in-Publication Data

Lucado, Max.
    The way home : a princess story / Max Lucado ; illustrated by
Tristen Elwell.
        p. cm.
    Summary: A beloved princess, adopted years ago as a
foundling, longs to travel beyond the castle walls where the
Lowlanders are said to play all the day long.
    ISBN 1-4003-0554-3 (hardcover)
    [1. Princesses—Fiction. 2. Kings, queens, rulers, etc.—Fiction.
3. Fathers and daughters—Fiction.] I. Elwell, Tristen, ill. II. Title.
PZ7.L9684Way 2005
[E]—dc22

                                                    2005014506

Printed in the United States of America
05 06 07 08 PHX 5 4 3 2 1

For our Brazilian princesses—
Paulina and Victoria Downing

ong, long ago, in a kingdom more majestic than any other, there lived a beautiful, young princess, Anna. Anna had not always been a princess. When she was an infant, the king had found her, abandoned in the forest, and brought her to the castle to raise as his own.

Yet as Anna grew, so did her curiosity. She wondered about the world outside the kingdom. What had she missed? What lay beyond the green gardens of the castle? Anna sighed. She propped her elbow on the ledge, rested her chin in her hand, and stared out the castle window.

Flowers dotted the meadow. Children splashed in the creek. Beyond the meadow, the dark forest loomed. What a beautiful day outside! What a bad day to be inside!

"Ahem! Princess," a voice called, "your studies."

"Yes, Sir Henry." Anna glanced again toward the forest. "Is it true?"

The round man looked up, raising his eyebrows. "Excuse me?"

"About the Lowlanders. I hear that they never work and their days are all filled with fun."

The tutor lowered his book. "Forget them! They mean us harm."

"But *all* I do is work. I'm just not sure I was meant to be a princess."

Sir Henry crossed the room and rested his hands on Anna's shoulders. "I have watched you since the day you arrived, and I have been your teacher since you were small. I have seen you blossom with your father's guidance. Listen to me. The forest is no place for anyone, especially the daughter of royalty. Those trees know an evil that does not sleep."

"But—"

Sir Henry interrupted by placing a finger on her lips. "Your studies. There is much to learn."

Anna nodded, but stole one last glance into the valley, wondering about life away from the castle.

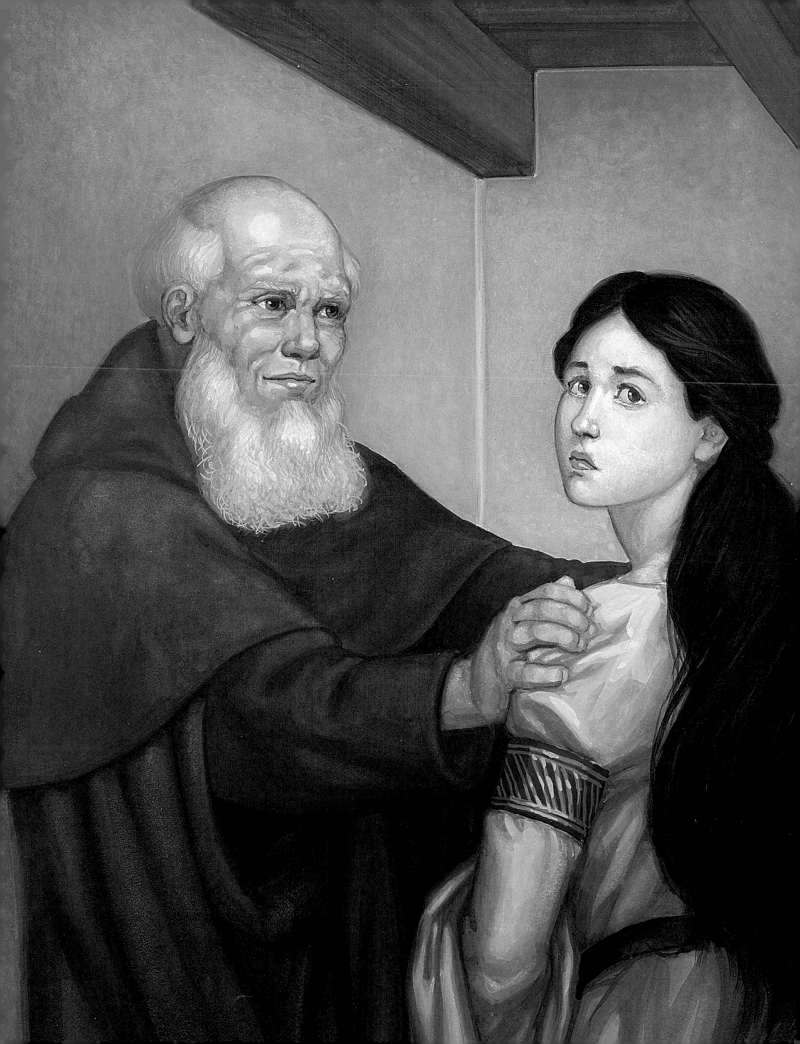

Deep within the forest, three Lowlanders plotted and rummaged through costumes.

Ima and Gunnah usually shared a costume.

"Let's be donkeys," Ima offered.

"Not again. That suit is hot, and you stink!" Gunnah smirked.

Getcha pulled on a hood. "The princess will feel sorry for a poor, old hag."

Passing as hags wouldn't be hard for them. With hunched shoulders and warty noses, they looked the part. They were tree-stump shaped, with faces as bumpy as cobblestones and ears as pointy as oak leaves.

Getcha was the tallest, but if he were to stand near the princess, he'd barely come up to her waist.

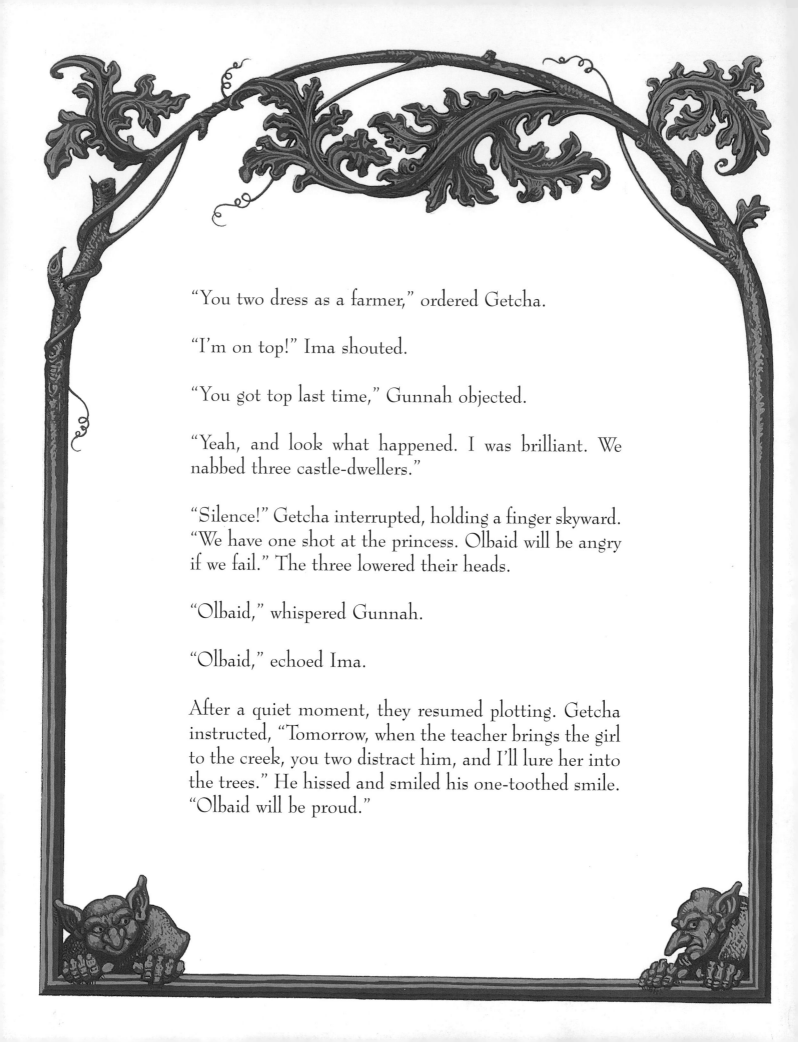

"You two dress as a farmer," ordered Getcha.

"I'm on top!" Ima shouted.

"You got top last time," Gunnah objected.

"Yeah, and look what happened. I was brilliant. We nabbed three castle-dwellers."

"Silence!" Getcha interrupted, holding a finger skyward. "We have one shot at the princess. Olbaid will be angry if we fail." The three lowered their heads.

"Olbaid," whispered Gunnah.

"Olbaid," echoed Ima.

After a quiet moment, they resumed plotting. Getcha instructed, "Tomorrow, when the teacher brings the girl to the creek, you two distract him, and I'll lure her into the trees." He hissed and smiled his one-toothed smile. "Olbaid will be proud."

Back at the castle, the king shook his head. "Why?!" he asked his daughter's teacher. "Why is she so curious about the Lowlanders?" He stroked his square jaw and stared at his old friend.

"Maybe she wonders what her life would have been like if she had not become a princess," Sir Henry explained. "She hears rumors of their easy life."

"Easy!? Dwelling in a dark forest? Dodging the wrath of Olbaid?"

"She is young, Your Majesty."

"Yes, but she is mine." The king shook his head. "I've tried to tell her so many times. She is meant to do important things."

"Perhaps she will listen to me, Your Majesty," Edward said, stepping forward.

The king smiled at the young man who spoke. Edward was the strongest of his knights. "Indeed she might listen to you, Edward. She certainly notices you."

Edward's face blushed, but he did not smile. "We must put an end to these thoughts of the Lowland. Olbaid sees your daughter as a prize to be won."

The king stiffened at the sound of his archenemy's name. "You're right. Talk to her. Tell her how they poison minds and . . ." He paused. "Remind her once more how much I love her."

Sir Henry led Edward through grand halls toward a large door. He heard feet pattering on the other side and shook his head knowing Anna was dashing toward her desk from the window. As they entered, she reopened her book.

Anna looked at Edward and smiled. Her beauty stole his breath: black satin hair, rosy cheeks, deep green eyes. It wasn't long ago that he had avoided her. During the time that he had trained to be a knight, she had excelled at being a brat. How was she so suddenly pretty?!

"Edward?" Sir Henry reminded.

"Oh yes," he answered, clearing his throat. "With your permission, m'lady?"

She nodded.

"Your fascination with the forest troubles us, Princess."

"Have you met them, Edward?" Her excited voice betrayed her curiosity.

"The Lowlanders mean you harm."

"But I've heard they have nothing but fun."

"You've heard wrong. Avoid these servants of Olbaid."

She shrugged, but the tone of Edward's next words urged her to heed his caution. "Your father loves you so much, Anna."

She smiled. "And I love him, Edward. I know to be careful."

The knight nodded with uncertainty and then dismissed himself. Still worried, he walked through the halls, fearing the worst. He was right to do so.

The next day, Sir Henry kept watch as the princess
waded in the creek. The blue sky and bubbling waters
lifted his spirits.

Suddenly a voice called, "Oh friend, help!"

The teacher turned to see a farmer ambling toward
him. The wide-brimmed hat and chest-length beard
covered Ima's face. Gunnah, hidden within the long
coat, groaned beneath the weight. Barely able to see,
he tripped, causing Ima to wobble even more.

The sight of the odd man might have roused Sir Henry's
suspicions, but the man's clumsiness stirred his
compassion. He hurried toward him, unaware of a
disguised Lowlander approaching the princess.

"Is it true what I hear, young woman? That you desire to visit the forest?"

Anna, knee-deep in the water, looked up with a trusting smile. "You know the Lowlanders?"

"Indeed I do."

The princess glanced toward her teacher, helping the old man. "But . . . I can't."

"It will take only a moment," the woman enticed, beckoning with a crooked finger.

Anna looked toward the castle, then back to the entrancing, little figure.

By the time Sir Henry had righted the clumsy farmer, the old woman had convinced Anna to follow her into the forest. "For just a peek," Getcha assured in his highest voice.

Only a few steps into the trees, Anna regretted her decision. She couldn't keep up with the woman. "This may be easy for you, but I'm too—"

"Too what?" Getcha snapped in his normal voice, turning with such speed that his hood flew off. Anna tried to scream, but couldn't. "Too tall? Too pretty? Too good for the Lowlanders? You're one of us now!" he proclaimed.

The princess turned to run, but the forest had closed behind her.

"Your king can't save you!" Getcha cackled, rubbing his hands together.

Meanwhile, Sir Henry and the villagers searched, but no one had seen where Anna had entered the forest.

The princess was gone.

When the king heard, he wept quietly. "Who took her?" he asked Sir Henry.

"I don't know," the teacher responded sadly.

Suddenly, Edward entered, pulling the farmer by the sleeve, leading him before the king. Gunnah, within the cloak, tripped on Edward's foot, sending the two imps sprawling.

The Lowlanders scurried to their feet. Edward drew his sword. The king motioned him back.

"Where did you take Anna?" the king demanded.

Ima snickered. "Take her? She went by choice."

"Liars!" defied Edward.

"Any evidence of resistance? She *wanted* to leave," Gunnah added.

The king shook his head sadly.

He knew the Lowlander spoke the truth.

And he knew that no one, except a Lowlander, could navigate the forest.

Would he ever see Anna again? His attendants assumed he wouldn't want to. To be kidnapped is one matter, but to *run away*?

He spun from the window and surprised them, "I will go after her."

Their response was quick. "But the forest?"

"I will cut a path."

"It is thick!"

"I am strong."

Silence hung. Finally, one knight dared: "But, she . . . has chosen them."

The king replied, "She has been my daughter much longer than she has been with them."

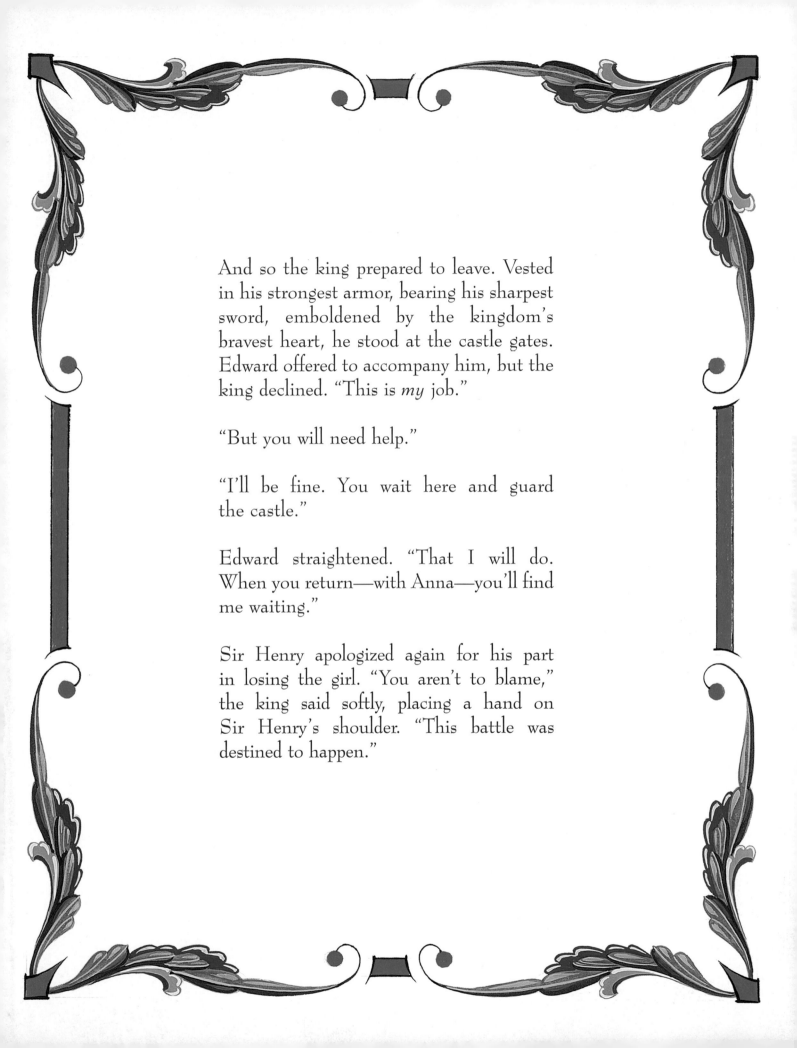

And so the king prepared to leave. Vested in his strongest armor, bearing his sharpest sword, emboldened by the kingdom's bravest heart, he stood at the castle gates. Edward offered to accompany him, but the king declined. "This is *my* job."

"But you will need help."

"I'll be fine. You wait here and guard the castle."

Edward straightened. "That I will do. When you return—with Anna—you'll find me waiting."

Sir Henry apologized again for his part in losing the girl. "You aren't to blame," the king said softly, placing a hand on Sir Henry's shoulder. "This battle was destined to happen."

People lined the castle walls, watching the king stride toward the trees. Without hesitation, he entered the forest, and with one mighty slash of his sword, ancient boughs began to tumble. The image of Anna crawling her way through the brushwood tormented him. His arms and legs bled from the thorns. Her cuts would be worse.

As the fog thickened, Lowlanders mounted resistance. Imps snapped at his legs. Swinging from above, they clawed his shoulders. Lacking courage to face him, they hid in the brush and darted from holes. One flash of the king's blade and they'd scamper into hiding. They could not slow his progress or lessen his resolve.

The forest ended abruptly. The king stepped into a clearing, his clothing and skin torn.

He found Anna, confused, in the center of the village. The forest dwellers had abandoned their huts. The princess didn't run, nor did she approach her father. She stood frozen with shame.

He sighed. Her clothing and skin were shredded, her hair matted and caught with burrs. Her back was already beginning to stoop like a Lowlander. When he touched her shoulder, she stiffened.

"Come back with me," he offered.

She said nothing.

"Why would you stay?"

She had no answer. Not for her father. Not even for herself.

"Come back to the castle with me," he offered.

"I'm one of them now," she mumbled.

"But you weren't made for this."

The king was silent. He knew what had to be done.

"Looking for me?" The sound of Olbaid's voice made the monarch cringe. "Your daughter is content here."

"No one is content in your presence."

Olbaid's eyes glowed. His bat-winged cape hung to the ground, exposing clawed feet.

"I have come for Anna."

"She is mine—one of many to come. They cannot resist. You can't keep them from the shadows," Olbaid growled.

"I'll give you something better," the king offered.

"What could be better than the daughter of the king?!" Olbaid laughed, then realized what the king meant. "You wouldn't!"

The king's silence was his answer.

"Give yourself?"

Anna turned toward her father. "No," she prayed softly.

Olbaid risked no delay. He opened his cape, releasing legions of Lowlanders that rushed to swarm the king.

Soon Olbaid stood over the king's lifeless body. "Behold your king, Anna. His love couldn't save you, nor himself."

Anna rushed to her father. Her tears dropped onto his face. "What have I done?"

Olbaid yanked her up. "You have sealed your people's doom." He cocked his head, releasing high-pitched laughter. The Lowlanders jumped, danced, and screamed at the feet of their leader.

Anna stood still. "What have I done?" she asked herself again. Kneeling, she took the king's hand and pressed it to her face.

Then, she felt his hand move.

She searched his face. For years, when retelling this story, she would describe this moment. His eyes opened and sparkled as if saying, "They may try, but they can't kill me."

She stood. Olbaid commanded, "Grab her!"

"Stop!" her father declared, jumping to his feet. "You have no power over me or mine."

The Lowlanders crept backward. Olbaid did too, muttering. He and his defeated followers ducked into the forest.

Just then, Ima and Gunnah appeared. "We escaped! Anna is ours—"

Ima stopped. Gunnah ran into him. They stared at the king, then at the empty village.

"Uh . . . looks like we came at a bad time," Ima whimpered, slowly backing away. The two turned and ran between the trees.

The king turned to Anna, smiled, and extended his hand in her direction.

She still didn't understand. "I can't go back. I don't know the way."

"But, Anna, that is why I came." For the first time, she saw the opening, a path leading to the castle. Now she understood.

Placing her hand in his and her trust in him, she made her choice.

"Stay with me," the father invited. "I'll show you the way home."